Contents

CIPS STUDY MATTERS

PROFESSIONAL DIPLOMA IN PROCUREMENT AND SUPPLY

REVISION NOTES

Programme and project management

© Profex Publishing Limited, 2012

Printed and distributed by:
The Chartered Institute of Purchasing & Supply, Easton House, Easton on the Hill, Stamford,
Lincolnshire PE9 3NZ
Tel: +44 (0) 1780 756 777
Fax: +44 (0) 1780 751 610
Email: info@cips.org
Website: www.cips.org

First edition December 2012

Preface

Welcome to your Revision Notes.

Your Revision Notes are a summarised version of the material contained in your Course Book. If you find that the Revision Notes refer to material that you do not recollect clearly, you should refer back to the Course Book to refresh your memory.

There is space at the end of each chapter in your Revision Notes where you can enter your own notes for reference.

A note on style

Throughout your Study Packs you will find that we use the masculine form of personal pronouns. This convention is adopted purely for the sake of stylistic convenience – we just don't like saying 'he/she' all the time. Please don't think this reflects any kind of bias or prejudice.

December 2012

CHAPTER 1

Key Aspects of Programmes and Projects

Programme management defined

Programme management: co-ordination and delivery of multiple interdependent projects which collectively deliver overall change and significant strategic benefits for the organisation.

Programme management challenges:

- Lack of top management ownership via programme board
- Facilitation of complex change
- Limited conception of what programme management entails (eg 'collection of projects')
- Cross-functional working and overcoming project 'silos'
- Co-ordination of individual projects into coherent and co-ordinated improvement process

Project management defined

Project: 'specific, finite task to be accomplished' with seven characteristics: importance, performance, finite due date, interdependencies, uniqueness, resources and conflict. (MM)

Project: 'unique, transient endeavour undertaken to achieve desired outcome' (APM) – NB different from 'business as usual'

Project management: 'process by which projects are defined, planned, monitored, controlled and delivered, such that the agreed benefits are realised' (APM)

Elements of project: Definition; Planning; Initiation; Control-key (Cost, Quality, Time), Organisational processes, Closure, Review/learning.

Project management challenges:

- Cross-functional working, different systems leading to challenge of co-ordination and leadership
- Finite resources
- Trade-offs between Cost, Quality, Time objectives
- Not 'business as usual': unknown elements, risk

Similarities and differences

Similar: create change; defined outcomes; delivery milestones; require co-ordinated resources; planning and control tools; CQT constraints; governance requirements; not 'business as usual'

Different: wider scope of programmes; higher-level change through programme scope and scale; higher-level governance of programmes; strategic nature of programmes.

Programme and project stakeholders

Stakeholders: individuals and groups who have legitimate interest or 'stake' in project.

Eg: client/commissioner, steering committee/board, project owner, project manager, project team, users, financers + secondary stakeholders (affected by project process/outcomes)

Stakeholder mapping (eg Mendelow power/interest matrix): used to identify interested/ influential stakeholders and strategies for stakeholder engagement and management.

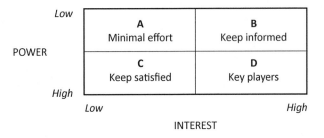

Stakeholder satisfaction = perception *minus* expectation: need to manage expectations and perceptions, through stakeholder communication

Stakeholder expectations eg: fitness for purpose, absence of defects, on-time delivery, VFM, reasonable running costs, satisfactory reliability and durability

Safety, quality, cost and delivery

'Iron triangle' (CQT Triangle): Cost, Quality, Time objectives, constraints, trade-offs

Safety: additional priority (eg in construction) and potential constraint (eg on time, cost).
- Health and safety of workers; legal obligations + costs of accidents + responsible purchasing (eg re child labour, enforced labour, overtime, conditions etc: ILO Conventions)
- Need to ensure vigilance and co-operation of managers, inspectors, workers

Constraints: trade-offs between CQTS objectives – within framework of stakeholder expectations and priorities.

Measurement and control:

- Costs: quantified, comparatively easy to measure and control: budgetary control
- Quality: tools designed for repetitive process work: project more complex (stakeholder perceptions of quality; changing priorities; potential for later rectification)
- Time: tools eg WBS, CPA – but need for combined time and cost measures (eg EVA: value of work by percentage completion)

Progress-tracking metrics (time): percentage complete values; estimated remaining durations; actual start and finish times – supported by project management software.

Reporting progress: simple measures; only critical factors measured; appropriate control limits; reporting by exception only.

Project success and failure

Greer (14 principles of project success): focus on CQT; planning: urgency; project lifecycle model; communication; evolve deliverables; sponsor sign-offs; document business need; fight for time to 'get it right first time'; match responsibility and authority; involve sponsors and stakeholders; sell project; acquire best people; prioritise

Pinto & Slevin (10 CSFs): mission; support from top management; project plan; client consultation; personnel; technical support; client acceptance; monitoring and feedback; communication; trouble-shooting.

Greer (10 ways projects fail): no priorities; passive stakeholders; committee focus on management processes; interrupted teams; lack of planning; unidentified stakeholders; lack of sponsor sign-off; mismatch responsibility and authority; vague deliverables; lack of formal charter.

Elements of programmes and projects

MM's 7 Project elements: importance; performance (defined deliverables); lifecycle with finite due date; inter-dependencies; uniqueness; resources (finance, personnel etc); conflict (stakeholder interests)

Hard (systems, structures, plans, resources) + Soft (people, negotiation, influence, culture)

Basic elements and terms:

- **Business case:** document recording justification for project: benefits, costs and impact
- **Constraints:** factors that will need to be considered during life of project that cannot be changed: eg deadlines, law and regulation, dependencies on other projects.
- **Critical path:** sequence of activities that must be completed on time for project to be completed on schedule.

- **Deliverable:** a tangible or intangible outcome of project execution.
- **Milestone:** key event during life of project, eg completing project deliverables or stages.
- **Scope:** overall definition of what project should achieve + specific description of results. (*Scope creep:* uncontrolled growth of project scope resulting from changes to requirement.)
- **Stakeholder:** parties with an interest in a project or affected by its deliverables.

Work breakdown structure

- **WBS:** hierarchical breakdown of activities that need to be performed to complete a project: basis for project planning.
- **Process for using WBS** (MM):
  - Capture all activities needed to complete work
  - Breakdown into hierarchy of levels: Phases (Level 1) → Project deliverables and related milestones (Level 2) → Activities (Level 3) → Tasks or 'work packages' (Level 4)
  - For each work package; identify responsibility for completion; and calculate cost and resource requirements
  - Aggregate information into project master schedule
  - Continually examine resource usage and timing in light of WBS.

OWN NOTES

OWN NOTES

CHAPTER 2

Relationships in the Supply Chain

Supply chain networks

Supply chain management: 'integration of business processes from end user through original suppliers of products, services and information that add value' (Lambert)

Supply base rationalisation: savings in operational + managerial relationship costs

Supply chain tiering: main contractors managing networks of subcontractors

Relationships with subcontractors

Responsibilities of main contractors

Privity: responsibility for actions and defaults of subcontractors lies with main contractor.

Subcontracting/assignment clause: purchaser has no authority to prevent main contractor subcontracting, unless express clause in contract.

Relationships between main contractor and subcontractor often adversarial due to eg:

- 'Paid when paid' clause (generally prohibited in construction contracts in UK)
- Squeezing of subcontractor margins to control cost escalation
- Specialist subcontractors consulted late in project design process

Nominated subcontractors

Purchaser may seek to nominate subcontractors (eg to ensure compatibility of materials and systems with infrastructure). In construction contracts, 'prime cost' or 'provisional sum' typically included to cover work carried out by nominated subcontractor.

- Main contractor may not feel the same sense of responsibility for subcontractors.
- Purchaser will take greater responsibility for co-ordination of work.
- Main contractors will limit liability for work performed by nominated subcontractors.

Liability of subcontractors

Challenge of agreeing liabilities under contracts

- Subcontractors typically impose limits to liability for losses arising from defective work.
- Need for indemnity scheme (eg MHH) to allocate risks in common areas.

Small and medium-sized enterprises (SMEs)

Trend towards demand aggregation, large contracts (economies of scale) + complex tender requirements, leading to barriers to participation by SMEs in large projects, a social sustainability issue.

Overcoming barriers: encourage main contractors to use SME subcontractors; 'meet the buyer' forums; published contractor lists; ensure on-time payment of subcontractors; openness to consortium bids

NB: ensure SME subcontractors are risk-assessed; restrict number of subcontractors on work sites (to minimise labour relations risk)

Consortiums and joint ventures

Purchasing consortium: 'two or more organisations collaborating on certain aspects of their spend in order to generate leverage and better value for money for all' (CIPS).

Joint venture: combination of firms collaborating to take on demands of complex contract.

- Pools resources (shared costs of tender/project) and commercial and technical expertise
- Preferred by purchasers (dealing with single organisation)
- BUT: adds risk and cost of relationship management between partners.

Types of joint venture:

- **Vertical:** partner activities tend to follow sequentially.
- **Horizontal:** partners carry out work in parallel.
- **Homogeneous:** partners operating in broadly the same industry (eg construction)
- **Heterogeneous:** partners operating in different industries or specialisms
- **SPV** ('special purpose vehicle') set up a legal entity created for project or programme, comprising finance, construction and facilities management companies.

Traditional and contemporary relationships

Traditional relationships: arm's length transactional purchasing; price-focused selection; more or less adversarial relations (based on competing for share of value gains); procurement role limited (in terms of value-added outcomes); main contractor liability for defects.

Contemporary relationships: long-term partnership; collaborative value addition and gain sharing; transparency for improved supply chain management; supply chain capability development; and competition between supply chains (not just firms).

Latham Report (1994): 'partnering includes teamwork between supplier and client, and total continuous improvement requiring openness between parties, ready acceptance of new ideas, trust and perceived mutual benefit'.

Egan Report (1998): 'working together to improve performance through agreeing mutual objectives, devising a way for resolving and disputes and committing to continuous improvement, measuring progress and sharing gains'.

Features of partnering in PPM:

- Problem/conflict resolution
- Continuous improvement over time (KPIs)
- Integrated supply chain networks (moved from one project to the next)
- Purchaser commitment to principles of partnering (flexibility re competitive tendering)
- Main contractor commitment to long-term subcontracting arrangements
- Early involvement of specialist subcontractors on designs and ease-of-build

Effective teamworking:

- Characterised by collaborative planning and problem-solving; mutual trust and openness; equitable gain and risk sharing; ongoing conflict resolution.
- Requires team-building: agreeing goals, roles, work methods and communication channels; resolving conflicts; developing identity and solidarity

Project partnering and strategic partnering

Project partnering: client and main contractor work together on a single project, usually after competitive award of project contract.

- Savings through collaborative working (eg potential for open book cost management)
- Assurance of VFM through competitive award
- CQTS targets for individual project

Strategic partnering: client and integrated supply team (eg consortium) work together on a series of projects to promote continuous improvement over time. (Framework agreement awarded to team for a period of time: individual projects priced within arrangement.)

- Promotes VFM through integration, target costing and incentives, fewer design changes, collaborative efficiencies, reduced disputes
- Early engagement and involvement of key members
- Selection of suppliers on value, capability and compatibility, not just price
- Commitment to continuous performance measurement, learning and improvement

Level of partnership depends on factors such as team integration; advisory support; stakeholder engagement; and CTQS control.

Supplier and customer excellence models

Indicate status of customer-supplier relationship + alignment of operational activities with vision and strategy (cf 'balanced scorecard')

Scoring perceptions on five core elements of relationship performance:

- Relationship (trust, communication, collaboration)
- Capability (performance; training and development resources; accreditations etc)
- Strategy (buy-in and alignment, reflected in capacity levels and resources)
- Quality and innovation (meeting specification on CTQS; proactive and continuous improvement approach)
- Financial status (VFM, audit reports, effective financial management)

OWN NOTES

OWN NOTES

CHAPTER 3

Key Resources for Programmes and Projects

Resource loading and levelling, multi-project scheduling

Allocating and scheduling resources for individual projects OR across multiple projects (eg construction, software development firms).

Problems with time scheduling

Causes of time overruns (Maylor): estimate uncertainty; safety margins (padding) in estimates allowing procrastination; expansion of work to fill time available; delays passed on in full, time savings wasted (Goldratt); multi-tasking increasing lead times

Resource loading and levelling

Resource loading: amount of resources schedule requires during specific time periods.

- Eg employee assigned to percentage of project; assigned other tasks until 100% utilised. Predict hours for year, assign tasks accordingly, source extra staff or contractors
- Avoid overallocation: allow flexibility for absences, over-expectation etc.

Resource levelling: planning efficient capacity utilisation; responding to changes in demand.

- Available resources matched to demands of projects in short term: projects not urgent delayed until resources available
- PM software: level resources and avoid or flag over-allocations, constraints
- Long-range capacity adjustments eg by recruiting staff, investing in equipment.

Avoiding overallocation: set realistic schedules; prioritise tasks and projects; link or group similar tasks for different projects; leave float or slack time; avoid 'fire fighting' culture.

Multi-project scheduling

Treat several projects as part of single large project OR treat independently.

Criteria: **resource utilisation** (avoiding peaks and troughs); **schedule slippage** (time of delivery past due date); **resource effectiveness** (utilisation of reources to achieve delivery).

Leading and managing projects

People (project teams + supply network) a key resource: need to be directed, motivated etc.

- Management: objective-setting, planning, organising, directing and controlling – can be exercised over processes, resources, projects etc
- Leadership: influence, vision, inspiration, motivation – can only be exercised over people

Management = coping with complexity vs Leadership = coping with change (Kotter) Management = efficiency (via routine) vs Leadership = effectiveness (via vision and judgement) (Bennis & Nanus)

Managerial roles – what managers actually do (Mintzberg): Interpersonal (figurehead; leader; liaison), informational (monitor, spokesperson, disseminator); and decisional (entrepreneur, disturbance handler, resource allocator, negotiator)

Management skills for PM: planning, co-ordination, organisation, control, PM tools.

Leadership skills for PM: communicate vision; inspire and motivate team; sell change.

Why encourage managers to become leaders for projects? Energise and support change; secure commitment; set direction (teamworking, co-ordination); develop contribution; meet autonomy needs of skilled and professional teams.

Critical chain methodology

Theory of constraints (TOC) (Goldratt & Cox): scheduling overruns arise from constraints or bottlenecks in processes.

- Identify constraint eg shortage of resource
- Exploit constraint: make best use of scarce resource
- Subordinate everything else to constraint: eg schedule around it
- Elevate (mitigate) constraint: find additional resources or alternatives.

Critical chain project management (CCPM): new approach to estimating times.

- Eliminate padding from time estimates: recognise 50% overrun, 50% earlier completion
- Build in single margin of safety (buffer) at final stage, not in individual activities
- Precedence relationships (sequenced activities) only an 'overview': flexibility required.

IT systems for project management

Increasing complexity + frequency of change in projects leads to a need for IT resources.

Advantages of PM software: fast, accurate, high-volume data processing; automatic re-calculation for changes; rapid, flexible management information; integrated multi-programme calculation and planning; standardisation for ease of use (eg layout of project plans).

Disadvantages of PM software: financial investment; limitations of software suites; need for user training; potential for user error; erosion of some types of expertise; may not allow for CCPM methodology.

Web-based applications: flexibility; controlled access; accessible by multiple users; no software installation requirement; version control and maintenance centrally managed

Communication systems:

- Synchronous (simultaneous): audio/video/web conferencing, instant messaging – real-time interaction for fast decision-making.
- Asynchronous (not simultaneous): online discussion boards, email, streaming audio/video, shared desktops and calendars – allow collaboration over extended period of time; no time-zone issues.

Asset finance and the role of banks

Project cashflow: negative in initial phases (high rate of 'cash burn')

Sources of project finance: cashflows of firm (surplus cash on deposit) + external funding:

- *Temporary cash deficit*: short-term unsecured bank loan ('signature loan') or short-term secured loan (using assets as collateral).
- *Long-term finance* for working capital or capital expenditures: debt or equity finance.

Debt finance: selling bonds, bills, or notes to investors (principally banks); repayment of loan principal (capital) + interest

- *Debt instruments:* raising of loans from banks, pension funds or insurance companies.
- *Senior debt:* lenders have right to claim ownership of assets in event of default (followed by creditors with *subordinated debt).*
- *Standby loans:* lender commitment to advance loan at specified terms on demand (to cover contingency) or at specified future date (eg when project is generating income).
- *Debentures:* medium-term or long-term debt format in form of bond, secured on borrower's assets, with fixed-rate interest.
- *Bundled projects:* financing for portfolio of projects which collectively meet lender's Acceptable Rate of Return criteria as commercially viable.
- *Refinancing and restructuring:* eg for better interest rates; consolidation; reduced repayments; reduced risk; freed-up cash.

Equity finance: raising capital from external investors (eg venture capitalists, business angels or crowd-funding) in return for eg share of future profits or ownership (shares).

- *Advantages:* funding committed to projects; avoid costs of debt.
- *Disadvantages:* raising is demanding, costly and time consuming; investors demanding of information; project team may lose managerial power.

OWN NOTES

CHAPTER 4

The Project Lifecycle

Perspectives on project lifecycles

Standard 'S'-shaped pattern (MM):

- **Start-up**: project manager selected, team assembled, initial resources allocated, work programme drawn up. **Slow.**
- **Middle**: work gets under way, resources deployed productively, peak effort. **Fast.**
- **Ending**: final threads drawn together. **Slow.**

Alternative patterns: stepped; single accelerating or decelerating curve; inverse 'S'.

Estimates of risk more prone to error in earlier phases (MM): as time progresses, less uncertainty as project deliverables 'in the bag'.

A four-stage PLC (Maylor)

PHASE	ACTIVITY	DESCRIPTION
D1: Define	*Conceptualisation*	Generate explicit statement of needs
	Analysis	What has to be provided to meet those needs – is it feasible?
D2: Design	*Proposal*	Show how those needs will be met through the project activities
	Justification	Prepare and evaluate financial costs and benefits from the project
	Agreement	Point at which go-ahead is agreed by project sponsor
D3: Deliver	*Start-up*	Gather resources, assemble project teams
	Execution	Carry out defined activities
	Completion	Time/money constraint reached or activity series completed
	Handover	Output of project passed to client/user
D4: Develop	*Review*	Identify the outcomes for all stakeholders
	Feedback	Put in place improvements to procedures, fill gaps in knowledge, document lessons for the future

A five-stage PLC (Weiss & Wysocki)

PHASE	ACTIVITIES	DELIVERABLES
Definition	State problem; identify goals; list objectives; obtain preliminary resources; identify assumptions/risks	Project overview
Planning	Identify project activities; estimate time/cost; sequence activities; identify critical activities; write project proposal	Work breakdown; project network; critical path analysis; project proposal
Organising	Obtain resources; recruit leader and team; organise project team; assign work packages	Criteria for success; work description; work assignments
Controlling	Define management style; establish control tools; prepare 'sit reps'; review project schedule; issue change orders	Variances from targets; situation reports; staff allocation
Closing	Gain client acceptance; install deliverables; document the project; issue final report; conduct review	Final report; audit; recommendations

Project initiation

Overview (clarified and agreed with stakeholders) of:

- **Objectives:** end result the project is trying to achieve, including CQT objectives.
- **Scope:** responsibilities covered by project management; work content and outcomes.
- **Strategy:** how PM will ensure that objectives will be met; phases and milestones.

Elements of project plan (MM): overview; objectives; general approach; contractual aspects; schedules; resources; personnel; risk management plans; evaluation methods.

Budget: capital and expense requirements; one-off costs separate from recurring costs. Sign-off to ensure required resources are available.

Organising projects and project implementation

Organisation: dividing work and responsibilities among project team and supply network.

Co-ordination: direction and alignment of different activities so that objectives are achieved.

Common pitfalls (Andersen *et al*): unclear responsibilities; lack of co-ordination; resources not available when required; people not motivated; managers not committed; poor communication; project manager lacking managerial skills.

Project structure: framework for responsibility and accountability, task and resource allocation, communication, monitoring and reporting, co-ordination, flexibility to changing demands, and social cohesion (motivator for members).

Inception: conclude contracting; mobilise resources; establish working relationships; hold 'kick-off' meeting; review and revise project plan

- Kick-off meeting: present project plan, assign responsibilities, gain commitment of team
- Handover from proposal team to implementation team (customer-contractor projects)
- Contract analysis workshop, engineering or design review meetings etc.

Implementation: deploy resources; implement activities; deliver results; monitor and review progress; review and revise project plan; report on progress

Co-ordination in project management

RACI matrix: who (individual or role) needs to be Responsible, Accountable, Consulted and Informed on each task and decision listed. One participation type generally assigned to each person – except that Accountable person may also be Responsible (for completing the task).

Project control

Three types of control system (MM):

- *Cybernetic:* measuring outputs, comparing with standard, reporting deviations, determining corrective action (negative feedback loop).
- *Go/No-go:* checking whether condition has been met: proceed to next step *or* stop and determine how to proceed (eg project gates, checkpoints and milestones).
- *Post-control:* post-completion review of objectives; deviations from milestones, checkpoints and budgets; final report on results; recommendations for performance and process improvement.

Change control: issuing change orders; logging and disseminating changes.

Project closure

Phase out: final reviews to maintain momentum; hand over deliverables; secure sign-off by client; ensure maintenance plans in place; ensure knowledge transfer; management lifecycle costs; communicate and celebrate successes; learn from experience; disband and re-allocate team

Documentation: evidence of completion; guidance for client on operation and maintenance of deliverables; learning for similar future projects. Ongoing logging of events should be part of activity schedule.

Final report: summary and evaluation of project performance; administrative performance; organisational structure; project and administrative teams; PM techniques used. Plus recommendations for improvement.

Project review

Project audit (independent internal auditor):

- Maylor: accounting systems (return on investment, cost variances); conformance to plan (customer satisfaction); quality procedures (customer perceptions); conformance to HR policy (team motivation); conformance to environment policy (impact assessment); conformance to plan (cost, techniques used); control systems (basis for improvement).
- MM: Current status; future status; status of crucial tasks; risk assessment; information for other projects; limitations of audit; lessons learned (experiential learning cycle).

OWN NOTES

OWN NOTES

CHAPTER 5

Contract Forms

The role of institutes and professional bodies

Model form contracts: sets of contract clauses that form a common template for the execution of work or projects in particular industries or contexts.

Advantages: contract terms well understood by parties; reduced timescales for negotiation and development; accessible legal expertise.

Disadvantages: differences in wording of terms; may not be directly applicable to situation; may be overly onerous for simple projects.

Examples of model form contracts

BODY	MODEL FORM CONTRACT
ICE	New Engineering Contract
IMechE/IET	Model form contract for supply of electrical, electronic or mechanical plan
IChemE	International form of contract: lump sum contract (International Red Book)
FIDIC	The Construction Contract
JCT	JCT Standard Building Contract

The New Engineering Contract

Created by Institution of Civil Engineers (ICE) to: standardise clauses covering different engineering specialisms involved in major projects; reduce adversarial relations in the construction industry; stimulate productive management; achieve clarity of terms and language; focus on core clauses (excluding specifics); clearly set out duties and responsibilities.

'A legal framework of project management procedures designed to handle all aspects of the management of engineering and construction projects. Its benefits – stimulus to good management, flexibility and simplicity – can be applied to any project, large or small' (ICE)

Suite of NEC3 contracts: Engineering and Construction Contract (ECC); Engineering and Construction Short Contract (ECSC); Engineering and Construction Subcontract (ECS); Engineering and Construction Short Subcontract (ECSS); Term Service Contract (TSC); Term Service Short Contract (TSSC); Professional Services Contract (PSC); Supply Contract (SC); Supply Short Contract (SSC); Adjudicator's Contract (AC); Framework Contract (FC).

NEC core clauses

- General (defined terms etc)
- Contractor's main responsibilities (provision of works, design, people, subcontracting)
- Time (start/end, key dates, acceleration provisions)
- Testing and defects (tests and inspections, notification, correction)
- Payment (and incentives)
- Compensation events (specified events for which contractor will be compensated for cost overruns)
- Title
- Risks and insurance (risk register; risk notifications; risk management; client's and contractor's risks);
- Termination

NEC optional clauses

Main option clauses (choice of pricing mechanism):

- Option A: priced contract with activity schedule
- Option B: priced contract with bill of quantities – lump sum contract approach
- Option C: target cost with activity schedule
- Option D: target cost with bill of quantities – financial risk shared in agreed proportions
- Option E: cost-reimbursable contract
- Option F: management contract (cost-reimbursable + margin)

Secondary option clauses:

- Price adjustment for inflation
- Changes in law (compensation event where they affect contractor's costs)
- Multiple currencies (currency risk borne by employer)
- Parent company guarantee
- Sectional completion (contractual rights over sections of works)
- Bonus for early completion
- Delay damages
- Partnering (KPIs linked to performance)
- Performance bond
- Advanced payment to contractor
- Limitation of contractor's liability

Other model form contracts

ICE terms:

- Contract pricing and control of work based on bills of quantities.
- Appointment of Engineer, acting as employer's agent in dealing with contractor(s)
- Contractor entitled to recover additional costs of dealing with contingencies.

FIDIC terms:

- Based on ICE contracts. Engineer as main decision-making authority
- Suite of model form contracts: range of contracting strategies.

JCT:

- Suite of contracts from major projects to minor works + framework agreements.
- Contracts generally let on basis of fixed lump sum pricing (subject to correction of errors, adjustment to scope of works by 'variation'); progress payments on certified completion of works.
- Encourage the use of retention monies: fixed percentage of contract sum withheld on interim invoices, for payment on completion (expiry of defects liability period).
- Encourage up-front agreement of liquidated and ascertained damages (LAD): estimate of weekly financial damages if contractor fails to meet milestones.
- 'Determination': contract can be terminated for failure of contractor to perform works according to contract (eg suspension of works, failure to correct defects)

Comparison of JCT and NEC

JCT	NEC
40 principal conditions	9 core clauses
Originally traditional contracts (expanded to include other procurement strategies)	Options accommodate all procurement strategies
Design consultant supervises contractor's work and applies contract conditions independently of employer and contractor	Project manager acts as the client's agent: not required to act independently
Reactive approach: consequences and actions determined in response to events	Proactive approach: designed to minimise problems, including early warning systems
Not focused on co-operative working style	Requires parties to act in spirit of mutual trust and co-operation
Claims dealt with retrospectively	Claims defined as 'compensation events' and dealt with during contract period

OWN NOTES

CHAPTER 6

Pricing Mechanisms

Fixed lump sum pricing

Continuum between two extremes:

- **Fixed price agreements:** schedule of fixed fees or payments agreed in advance (supplier bears all risk of cost variances)
- **Cost-plus agreements:** fixed percentage added to supplier's cost of production or delivery (buyer bears all the risk of cost variances)

Pricing arrangements, showing risks to buyer (Lysons & Farrington)

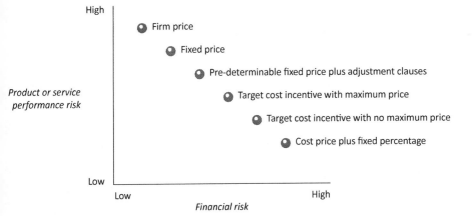

Fixed lump sum contracts

Contractor is paid agreed amount for fixed piece of work (eg *turnkey* or *design and build* contracting strategy)

- Price can be altered if variations (employer's liability) affect costs
- Progress payments can be linked to achieved milestones.
- Specification accuracy important: basis for contract.

Advantages for purchasers: high certainty re project cost; supplier bears risk of cost fluctuation; cashflow management; supplier motivation (incentive to complete work on time); administrative simplicity

Disadvantages: contractors maximising claims and variations to claw back costs; risk of 'corner cutting'

Fixed price with review or re-determination clauses

Contract provides that at end of specified period, or at specified intervals, price will be amended or opened to review, in light of cost fluctuations, performance and contingencies.

May be suitable where parties are unable to agree on accurate or fair fixed price for duration of long-term contract: costs volatile, scope changing etc.

Bills of quantity

Bill of Quantity (BOQ): list of items of work + estimated quantities

Contractors tender unit prices for each item: contract price is sum of quoted prices × quantity actually used

'Measurement' of actual quantities used (by Standard Method of Measurement)

Variations and errors corrected in BOQ, a 'compensation event' (under NEC), leading to flexibility.

Creation of BOQ requires:
- Detailed plans for project; specification of materials; costs of materials
- Compounding of labour and material costs: combined into single rate, adjusted in regard to material quantities (absorption costing).

Activity schedule pricing

Purchaser provides contractor with description of requirement (outcome- or performance-based specification), leading to programme of work.

Each activity (eg Gantt chart bar) is priced: contractor paid for each completed activity at assessment date following completion.

Advantages: maximum flexibility for contractor solutions; requires contractor pre-planning; payments linked to completion (greater risk owned by contractor; more purchaser certainty).

Target costing methods and risk and reward pricing mechanisms

Target costing

Target cost (likely result under 'normal' business conditions) established for project: deviations in actual costs shared between contractor and purchaser on pre-agreed formula.

Depending on confidence in target cost estimate, limitations or maximum/minimum fees can be agreed.

- **Target cost with maximum price**: contract stipulates target price (based on target cost, including agreed profit margin) *and* a maximum or ceiling price for the contract. Excess costs are borne by the supplier; cost savings are shared on agreed formula.
- **Target cost without maximum price**: contract stipulates target price (based on target cost) with no price 'ceiling' to protect buyer. Excess costs *and* savings are shared on an agreed basis.

Suitable where: scope or specification is not easy to define over life of contract; flexibility required; purchaser and contractor can contribute to decreasing cost; and desirable to share risks.

Other incentive or incentivised contracts

- Target cost for supply: savings shared with purchaser on agreed proportion basis
- Staged payments or contingency payments
- Bonus payments (or incentive fees) added to fixed price
- Revenue, profit or gain sharing

Cost-reimbursable contracts

Buyer agrees to reimburse supplier for all allowable, allocable and reasonable costs incurred in performing the contract *plus* a fixed fee or percentage representing supplier's profit.

Cost plus fixed fee (CPFF): payment of allowed costs *plus* fixed amount for work (varied only if scope changes). Used for uncertain contracts with few options (eg R&D).

Cost plus incentive fee (CPIF): payment of allowed costs *plus* higher fee for exceeding targets. Used to incentivise suppliers (eg reduce costs, establish standards)

Cost plus award fee (CPAF): payment of allowed costs *plus* bonus for 'effort in meeting buyer's needs'. Used for services (eg design or software development) where desirable to reward non-quantitative aspects of performance.

Cost without fee: for non-profit-making providers (eg university research units)

Cost sharing: where supplier stands to benefit from own work (eg R & D)

Time and materials: for contracts (eg repair services) where precise work cannot be predicted in advance: agreed fixed rate per labour hour *plus* materials supplied at cost.

Generally less advantageous to buyer: risk of cost fluctuations; lack of supplier motivation; need to scrutinise supplier cost schedules. BUT: final cost may be less than fixed price contract, as supplier does not have to inflate price to cover risks.

OWN NOTES

OWN NOTES

CHAPTER 7

Contracting Options

Client co-ordinated approaches to major projects

Project management strategy

Internal resources or external contractors? Four options (Marsh):

- Traditional client co-ordinated
- Full turnkey
- Partial turnkey
- Management contracting

Client co-ordinated contracting

Client responsible for design of project works. Responsibility of external contractors limited to performing assigned work 'packages' in line with client design and specification. Client controls project through consultant or project manager.

Advantages: best value (packages awarded on competitive tender); client retains total control.

Disadvantages: lack of early contractor involvement (expertise in design, process); main contractor has no sense of ownership; lack of communication between contractors.

EPC/design and build forms of contract

Full turnkey contracting

'Turnkey' = **'Design and Build'** = 'Engineering Procurement and Construction' (EPC)

Client specifies requirement. Contractor takes 'single-point' responsibility to design and deliver project to client's requirements.

Usually used for straightforward construction projects.

Advantages: single-point responsibility; quick completion; encourages design innovation; avoids diseconomies of multiple contractors; minimises claims for 'extras'

Disadvantages: disastrous if unsuitable contractor; limited choice of contractors; price reflects high risk and responsibility of contractor; contractor may skimp (beyond strict conformance).

'**Develop and construct**': client has design prepared to concept design stage: contractor responsible for completing design and carrying out construction.

Partial turnkey contracting

Client and contractor agree on division of responsibilities.

- Activities not assigned to turnkey contractor carried out by client or additional (separately appointed) contractors: client responsible for co-ordinating work.
- Designs 'novated' to contract with main contractor: contractor responsible for construction *but* limited liability for problems with design (liability with contracting party eg consultants).

Advantages: turnkey advantages + opportunity to contract separately for additional activities (lower price, wider choice of suppliers)

Disadvantages: client interferes in contractor's performance of work; problems in client's performance impact on contractor activity.

Management contracting and construction management

Management contracting: client appoints external organisation to manage and co-ordinate design and construction phases.

- Management contractor lets contracts for design, construction and installation work to specialist subcontractors: focuses on project management.
- Management contractor paid defined costs: actual cost of works and subcontractors + fee. Liability for breach limited to amount(s) recoverable from defaulting subcontractor(s).

Construction management: works contracts let directly by client, but *managed* on behalf of client by construction management company (professional project manager).

Advantages: savings in project duration and costs (design evolves together with engineering); co-ordinated teamwork; fewer variations to contract

Disadvantages: project manager caught between demands of client and subcontractors; client will not know full expected cost at outset (only estimates of project manager).

Design, build, operate and ownership forms of contract

'BOOT' (Build, Own, Operate, Transfer):

- Concession granted by **principal** (eg government) to **promoter** (eg construction contractor or consortium) for a defined period: 'concession agreement'
- Promoter responsible for construction, financing, operation and maintenance of facility: collects revenues from operation to recoup costs and make a margin of profit
- End of concession: transferred at no cost to principal, as fully operational facility.

Eg road infrastructure, pipeline, power, healthcare facilities

Work packages:

- *Construction:* land purchase, design, construction, supervision, insurances, legal etc
- *Operational:* facilities management services, training, supplies, insurances, licences etc
- *Financial:* funding (bank loan, shareholder agremenets with investors)
- *Revenue:* pricing for services, demand and capacity management, taxation etc.

Concession period: sufficient to allow promoter profit – but not excessive profits. Eg 10–15 years for infrastructure projects.

Variations: FBOOT (finance, build, own, operate, transfer); BOO (build, own, operate); BOL (build, operate, lease); DBOM (design, build, operate, maintain); DBOT (design, build, operate, transfer); BOOST (build, own, operate, subsidise, transfer); BTO (build, transfer, operate); BOT (build, operate, transfer).

Advantages: additionality; credibility; efficiencies; benchmark; technology transfer; privatisation; off-balance-sheet financing (capital investment not from public sector)

Disadvantages: corner-cutting by promoter; lower standards of CSR; non-viability for promoter; risks of project failure; costs of finance over long term.

Public private sector partnerships

Public Private Partnerships (PPP): making best use of private and public sector skills, ensuring better value in provision of public services.

- Introduction of private sector ownership into state-owned functions via range of structures (eg flotation or strategic partnering)
- Public sector contracting to purchase quality services on a long-term basis: using private sector management skills, incentivised by financial investment (eg PFI)
- Partnership arrangements where private sector expertise and finance are used to exploit commercial potential of government assets (eg back-office partnerships).

Advantages: private sector finance, skills and capacity; additionality (larger and more complex projects possible); shared risk; off-balance-sheet finance; potential for (incentivised) continuous improvement

Disadvantages: private sector contractor making insufficient or excessive profits; substantial bidding costs (legal recourse if project not pursued); HR issues (public service staff transferred to private sector); 'corner cutting' to maximise profit.

PPP models

Government-Owned, Contractor-Operated (GOCO) eg for critical or unique facilities:

- Private sector develops facility, but public agency retains title to asset.
- Private sector investment safeguarded (eg minimum compensation if early termination)

Private Finance Initiative (PFI): accessing private sector finance for projects.

- *Financially free-standing:* private sector recovers costs through revenue from operation
- *Services sold to public sector:* private sector charges authority for services provided
- *Joint venture:* project partly publically funded, but under private sector control.

Design, Build, Finance, Operate (DBFO): private consortium designs, constructs, finances, operates and maintains a public sector asset for a period of years – as in BOOT.

Risk management and transfer within PPP

Risks associated with PPP/PFI: design and construction; commissioning and operating; demand; final residual value; technology and obsolescence; regulation and compliance; project finance; contractor default

PPP project should ensure all risks allocated to party best able to manage them at least cost: 'optimal risk transfer'

Essential to identify, evaluate, monitor and be transparent about risks: risk register.

Objectives (HM Treasury): common understanding of main risks; consistent approach to pricing across similar projects; reduction in project time and cost (standard approach).

OWN NOTES

OWN NOTES

CHAPTER 8

Investment Appraisal

The purpose of investment appraisal

Capital investment: high value, long asset life; hence importance of evaluating investment decision + challenge balancing up-front expenditure and future costs and benefits.

Project cashflows:

- Outflows (cost of equipment, loan interest, wages and salaries, tax)
- Inflows (revenue, savings in operating costs, reduced tax, grants, disposal of asset)
- Net cashflows (cash inflows *minus* cash outflows for period): typically negative in early years, positive later (as operating benefits take effect)
- Opportunity costs of capital (benefit forgone by investing in project A rather than B).

Investment decision: positive cashflow potential; comparative value of alternative projects; timing of cashflows (payback period).

Appraisal techniques: payback; average rate of return (ARR); discounted cashflow (DCF).

Payback analysis

Assess how long a project will take to 'pay back' initial investment.

Eg: Purchase of £200,000 machine leading to financial benefits of £50,000 pa over 5 year use.

	Net cashflow each year £	Cumulative cashflow £	
Year 0	(200,000)	(200,000)	**Negative cashflow only partly offset**
Year 1	50,000	(150,000)	
Year 2	50,000	(100,000)	
Year 3	50,000	(50,000)	**Investment paid back**
Year 4	50,000	0	
Year 5	50,000	50,000	**Positive cashflow**

Advantages: simple to use; relatively 'safe' (recoup 'quickly': benefits not too speculative); useful for preliminary screening of potential projects (eg adopt only if payback within 10 years)

Disadvantages: doesn't look at rate of return (profitability), only rapidity of repayment.

The average rate of return (ARR) method

Calculate average rate of return earned by money invested.

Eg:

- Overall rate of return (£200,000 invested; £250,000 savings) = £50,000
- Average return (over 5 years) = £10,000 = 5% rate of return on £200,000 invested.

Advantages: easy to compare ARR for different projects to identify project offering *best rate of return* (may be more relevant than payback period); useful as preliminary criterion for evaluation

Disadvantages: doesn't look at project life (15% for 5 years may be better than 20% for 2 years); doesn't look at cashflow timing (later flows – more speculative – given equal weight); measurement of accounting profits is subjective.

Principles of discounted cashflow

The time value of money:

- Preference for *receiving money now rather than later,* because of risk, inflation eroding value, interest adding value (invested now).
- Preference for *paying money in future, rather than now* (eg because interest being earned).

Present value:

- Calculate value in today's terms (*present value)* of money receivable or payable at future date: eg *discount* for % interest lost or gained.
- Cashflows arising in future are *discounted* to arrive at present value.

Discount:

- Present value of a future sum of money depends on **discount rate** and **how far in future** money will be paid or received.
- Rate used depends on **cost of capital**. *Simple:* intrest rate on loan finance. *More complex:* weighted average cost of capital (WACC).
- **DCF tables:** read off both factors (per £1 receivable or payable). Eg: £1,000 receivable in 2 years at 5%: present value = £907.

			Rate of discount			
Year	5%	6%	7%	8%	9%	10%
0	1.000	1.000	1.000	1.000	1.000	1.000
1	0.952	0.943	0.935	0.926	0.917	0.909
2	0.907	0.890	0.873	0.857	0.842	0.826

Net present value (NPV):

- Discount estimated **net cashflows** for each year > **total present values** of all cashflows over life of project (NPV).
- *Positive NPV:* project is worth undertaking OR *Negative NPV:* project costs more than it is worth.
- Project *comparison:* higher NPV is more attractive.

Year	Disc rate @ 8%	Project A Cashflows £	Present value £	Project B Cashflows £	Present value £
0	1.000	(200,000)	(200,000)	(200,000)	(200,000)
1	0.926	50,000	46,300	20,000	18,520
...	...	...	...	...	...
6	0.630		80,000		50,400
NPV			(350)		15,220

Advantages of DCF:

- Takes account of all cashflows over product life (unlike payback method)
- Focuses on most relevant factor: cashflow (unlike ARR: accounting profit or loss)
- Takes account of time value of money (unlike other methods

Disadvantages of DCF:

- Calculations based on subjective assumptions
- Future cashflows uncertain in amount (increasingly, as time horizon lengthens)
- Practical difficulties of determining appropriate discount rate

Calculating the internal rates of return

Internal rate of return (IRR) = **% discount rate at which NPV = 0**

- If firm can borrow at % *less than IRR:* IRR (return) = greater than cost of financing **(target/hurdle rate)**: project will be viable.
- Eg: NPV @ 4% = £2,000, NPV @ 6% = −£2,000: IRR = 5%.

If hurdle rate (cost of finance) = 4%, project should be accepted.

Using IT for investment appraisal

- Spreadsheet software available for DCF calculations
- Sensitivity analysis to explore impact of changes in variables (eg costs, revenues): plan for contingencies, uncertainty
- Access to information (eg via internet): eg lending rates, foreign exchange rates, industry costs, business analysis

OWN NOTES

CHAPTER 9

Structures for Corporate Governance

Project boards/executive

Corporate governance: ensuring that projects and programmes deliver results effectively, ethically and legally, via mechanisms for process, accountability, oversight, control, reporting, stakeholder relations, risk management, probity.

Programme board

High-level, strategic governance; overseeing entire programme; identifying and resolving cross-cutting issues (eg sustainability or stakeholder relations)

Terms of reference: scope of remit, objectives, operating methods (programme board terms of reference cascaded down to project boards, with own subsidary terms of reference)

Skill composition: skills for relevant delivery elements and themes + skills in relationship management and negotiation.

Roles: chair; programme director or manager; sub-programme or project managers (reporting by exception); key stakeholders; programme management team. (May be sub-groups or steering groups to deal with specific areas.)

Balance of oversight: board should only intervene in projects on significant issues (affecting programme) BUT must ensure that issues are escalated from project level where necessary.

Project board

Champion project to organisation and stakeholders

Provide overall guidance and direction to project

Support Project Manager in decision-making process

Report to senior management groups

Approve project plans (but challenge plans and estimates)

Take 'ownership' of appropriate identified project risks and take action to mitigate risks.

Project responsibility charting

RACI (Responsible, Accountable, Consulted, Informed) matrix – suitable for smaller projects.

Project responsibility charting: derivative of RACI – suitable for larger projects. Charts:

- *Milestones*
- *Companies or departments* involved
- *Roles and responsibilities* of companies or departments against each milestone:

Executes; takes sole or ultimate decision; takes joint or part decision; manages progress; provides tuition; must be consulted; must be informed; available to advise.

Used at three levels: global or programme level (companies and work packages and milestones); organisational level (activities and departments); micro level (tasks and individuals).

The use of project initiation documents

Project selection (MM)

Non-numerical: sacred cow (championed by senior figure); operating necessity; competitive necessity; product line extension; comparative benefit.

Numerical:

- Financial appraisal: project justified on profitiablity (eg payback, ARR, DCF);
- Unweighted factor model: list of evaluation criteria, score project on number satisfied
- Unweighted factor scoring model: add weighting for *how closely* project matches criteria
- Weighted factor scoring model: add weighting for *importance* of criteria satisfied

Project initiation

Exchange of project brief and PID

- Purchaser prepares project brief, specifying the deliverables required.
- Project organisation replies with project initiation document (PID).

Content of PID: project goals and objectives; CSFs; project scope; risk assessment; roles and responsibilities; control mechanisms; reporting; milestones; budget

Statement of Work (SoW): statement of work and deliverables the project must produce. Used to direct work of internal teams + suppliers.

Structures of project management

Pure project structure: project team a self contained unit: PM with full authority over project; project team directly responsible to PM.

- *Advantages* (MM): accountability; cross-functional communication; development and consistency of expertise; identity (fosters commitment); decision-making authority; unity of command; simplicity and flexibility; supports systems-based approach.

- *Disadvantages:* duplication of personnel; loss of generalist expertise; silo mentality; competition with mainstream organisation.

Functional structure: project assigned to functional unit with specialism or interest; cross-functional communication and collaboration where required.

- *Advantages* (MM): flexibility in use of staff; access to specialist technical knowledge; base of continuity; path of development for experts
- *Disadvantages:* conflict with ongoing work of host function; orientation to specialism rather than problem-solving; challenges of cross-functional collaboration.

Matrix structure: hybrid where functions provide staff on full-time or part-time basis to project team, which draws from different functions.

- *Advantages:* functional efficiency + project accountability; fosters cross-functional collaboration; tolerance of flexibility; highlights conflicts of authority
- *Disadvantages:* competition between functional and project management; stress of competing demands; inefficiency of ambiguous priorities and multi-tasking; slower decision-making

Project reporting

Highlight reports submitted regularly by project manager to steering committee or project board.

- Main mechanism of regular feedback control: monthly (or at intervals agreed at project initiation).
- Progress reports: brief summaries of status of project re schedule, budget, deliverables.

Checkpoints: progress review meetings for project teams, often held weekly (more frequently than highlight reports) for continuous monitoring by team members and leaders.

Reports at **milestones** (key stage targets) and **gates** (measurement points where each stage of work 'passes' or 'fails' against acceptance criteria).

End stage assessments, at completion of each stage of a project: reports from project manager and representatives of sponsor and user groups. Plans for following stage reviewed and approved, and management issues raised if necessary.

Project budgets, Gantt charts, critical path analysis (etc): used to report progress against specific quality, cost and schedule targets.

PM software may be used to co-ordinate progress tracking and reporting data.

Completion and post-completion reporting: project manager produces completion report, summarising project objectives and outcomes achieved; budget and schedule variances; and any ongoing issues or unfinished business (and how these will be followed up); etc.

OWN NOTES

CHAPTER 10

Objectives of Programmes and Projects

Identifying goals and objectives of projects

Clear objectives needed to ensure that purchasing project is implemented to the required timescales; achieving desired level of output or performance; within agreed budget.

Need for post-completion review to analyse whether objectives achieved, eg re: budget; performance achieved; customer satisfaction; delivery timescale; management effectiveness; supply relationships developed.

Latham Report criticised lack of **clearly defined objectives** in construction projects eg: VFM; pleasing to look at; free from defects on completion; delivered on time; fit for purpose; supported by worthwhile guarantees; reasonable running costs; satisfactory durability.

The balance between cost, quality and time in projects

Iron Triangle (CQT Triangle): See Chapter 1.

Relative importance and priority depends on:

- **Type of project** (Slack, Chambers and Johnson): eg quality (new aircraft); cost (fixed-grant research); time (entertainment event)
- **Stage of project lifecycle**: performance priority at start-up (achieve technical requirements); cost priority (as costs accumulate); time priority towards completion (pressure to complete by due date).

Trade-offs: eg schedule brought back on track by additional resources (impact on cost) or cutting corners (impact on quality, safety)

Need to balance priorities within policy + agreed outcomes + stakeholder expectations.

10

Technology project development

Importance of concise, accurate, clear, non-restrictive specification.

Problems in developing specification: lack of stakeholder communication; fast-changing requirements; unknown or innovative requirements; poor understanding of trading environment.

Move away from conformance-based (design, input) specifications towards performance-based (output, outcome) specifications: maximum flexibility for supplier expertise, solution development, innovation.

Innovation

Innovation: inventions, new technology and processes, adaptations, ideas for improvement.

Procurement techniques to stimulate supply chain innovation:

- Early supplier involvement (or early cross-functional dialogue) and partnering
- Performance-based specifications (to allow flexibility in developing best solutions)
- Support for SME contractors or subcontractors
- Evaluating variant bids and value outcomes; contract for IP rights
- Supplier development, continuous improvement agreements, risk-reward sharing
- Innovation councils, or cross-functional innovation steering groups

Building sustainability into major projects

Sustainable development: 'Development that meets the needs of the present without compromising the ability of future generations to meet their own needs.' (WCED)

Three-dimensional sustainability: economic, social, environmental (Profit, People, Planet)

Sustainable procurement: 'A process whereby organisations meet their needs for goods, services, works and utilities in a way that achieves value for money on a whole-life basis: generating benefits not only to the organisation, but also to society and the economy, whilst minimising damage to the environment.' (Sustainable Procurement Taskforce)

Aims of sustainable procurement:

- Minimise negative impacts of goods, works or services across lifecycle and through supply chain
- Minimise demand for non-renewable resources
- Apply fair contract prices and terms (ethical, human rights and employment standards)
- Promote diversity and equality throughout the supply chain.

Sustainability impacts of projects:

- **Waste hierarchy:** Rethink need; Reduce usage; Re-use; Recycle; Recover energy; Responsible disposal

- **Environmental impacts:** Depletion of non-renewable resources; energy use; carbon/ GHG emissions; pollution, waste and emissions; destruction of habitats and biodiversity; product and packaging waste to landfill etc.
- **Socio-economic impacts**: occupational illness and accidents; lack of diversity and equal opportunity; lack of community involvement and investment; barriers to SME participation; loss of employment; exploitation of child, forced or vulnerable workers; failure to pay living wage (or support supply chain in doing so).

Environmental standards: eg Building Research Establishment Environmental Assessment Methodology (BREEAM): rating for sustainable building design, construction and operation

Social standards: eg Social Accountability SA 8000 standard (based on ILO Conventions) – especially for projects and supply chains in developing or vulnerable economies:

- Elimination of child and forced labour
- Health and safety provision
- Freedom of association and collective bargaining
- Elimination of discrimination
- Responsible disciplinary practices
- Responsible and legal working hours
- Sufficient and legal remuneration
- Supply chain management systems.

Case study example: construction of Olympic Village, London 2012. Objectives re: carbon emissions, water use, waste minimisation, environmentally and socially responsible materials, protection of biodiversity and ecology; pollution; supporting communities; transport and mobility; disabled access; employment and business opportunity; health and wellbeing; stakeholder inclusion.

Impact on the community for major projects

Compliance with ILO conventions, ETI base code, SA 8000 and other minimum standards on human and labour rights – especially for projects involving vulnerable producers, workers and host communities

Impacts of major projects on host communities:

- Employment opportunities, possible distortion of employment patterns
- Usage, re-designation, degradation or reclamation of land
- Aesthetics, heritage values and amenities of build environment and infrastructure
- Destruction of arable land, habitats, biodiversity (eg as a result of construction)
- Traffic congestion, noise, vibration and emissions
- Waste, pollution, noise, emissions from project activities
- Usage of amenity, disruption of community lifestyles (eg fly-in-fly-out workers)
- Involvement (or lack of involvement) of community stakeholders: concerns, needs
- Opportunities for community investment, support and activity (eg sponsorships, infrastructure development).

Communicating project objectives to the supply chain

Market dialogue or market sounding with contractors and suppliers to promote opportunities for innovation in projects: eg open supplier meetings or forums

E-tendering systems to broadcast opportunities and provide project information

Invitations to tender, specifications, contracts, KPIs, project initiation document etc communicate project objectives

Standards, codes of conduct, best practice frameworks, benchmarks, etc

Project review meetings, contract management etc to reinforce objectives (and progress or problems in meeting them)

OWN NOTES

OWN NOTES

CHAPTER 11

Managing Risk

Risk: degree of uncertainty; probability of unwanted outcomes happening (CIPS)

Risk management: process whereby organisations methodically address risks attaching to activities, with the goal of achieving sustained benefit' (*Institute of Risk Management*)

Identifying assumptions and risks

Project risk

Projects may be highly speculative, unique, one-off: high degree of uncertainty

Capital projects: characterised by high investment and long lifecycle: greater risks of financing (eg timing of cashflows); contingencies and changes over lifecycle

Projects may be large, complex and impacting on stakeholders/communities (eg public works)

Multi-stakeholder, multi-collaborator enterprises: multiplication of risk and challenges of risk management (eg un-owned, un-monitored risk events, complex liability)

Interdependency of activities: risk events impact throughout project network and schedule

May involve high-risk work sites (construction activity, machinery) and logistics (remote locations, security of transport and storage of supplies etc)

Subject to changes in design, changes in specification, contractual disputes

Project failure risks

RISKS	CONTROL/MITIGATION
• Schedule variance (missed deadline) • Cost and budget variances • Team relationship breakdown • Lack of co-ordination, planning • Resistance from stakeholders • Environmental threats • Penalties for failure to fulfil deliverables • Changes to plan or specification leading to confusion and conflict	• Clear governance structure • Stakeholder management • Project planning and control tools (eg CPA, Gantt) • Defined milestones, stage reviews • Risk monitoring and management (risk register etc) • Contract development (risk/liability etc) • Contingency planning, managed changes • Early procurement and contractor involvement • Project review, learning and follow-up

11

The project risk management cycle

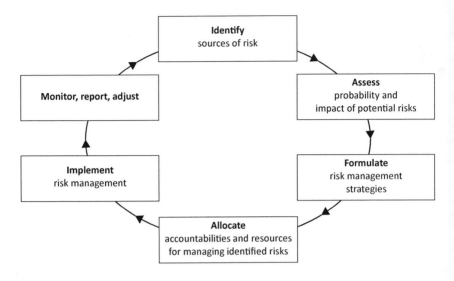

Risk identification *(What could go wrong?)*

Examine planning tools for vulnerabilities in structures and processes (eg WBS, critical path networks, process flowcharts, RACI)

Formal risk assessments, audits, inspections, documented in risk register

Stakeholder feedback and ideas (eg brainstorming, surveys, workshops)

Risk assessment/evaluation *(How likely? How bad?)*

Risk = Likelihood of occurrence of risk event × Severity of impact/consequence of risk event (eg scored 1–10)

Significant	Considerable management required	Must manage and monitor risks	Extensive management essential
Moderate	Risk may be worth accepting with monitoring	Management effort worthwhile	Management effort required
Minor	Accept risk	Accept, but monitor risk	Manage and monitor risk
	Low	*Medium*	High

LIKELIHOOD

Quantifying risk allows project manager:

- To prioritise risk management resources to most severe risks
- To set risk thresholds at which risk mitigation action will be triggered

Risk response *(What can we do about it?)*

Tolerate: 'live with it'. May be adequate for low-level risk, given competing use for resources.

Treat: risk control (active steps to minimise risk) or risk avoidance (alter variables to remove risk). May create acceptable residual risk – but at cost.

Transfer or share: eg allocation of responsibility to deliver, insurances, liability clauses and liquidated damages in contracts. Reduces exposure – at a cost.

Terminate: avoid risk by not engaging in project. Avoids risk – at cost of opportunity.

Contingency plan for high-impact risk: alternative courses of action, work-arounds and fallback positions.

Risk reporting *('What happened? What can we learn?')*

Monitoring and reporting of risk (eg risk registers and logs) allows the project manager:

- To be aware when project risk profile may be changing
- To gain assurance that risk management is effective – or to adjust plans as required
- To gather feedback for process improvement and future risk assessment

Tools and techniques eg: risk registers and logs (defined accountabilities for monitoring and management); audits; quality assurance systems; knowledge management and learning

Risk simulation

Stems from **sensitivity analysis**: used to determine how different values of one variable will impact on another (eg how wet weather will impact on progress of a works contract).

Monte Carlo simulation:

- Computerised modelling of different risk scenarios using quantitative analysis.
- Based on use of normal and Poisson distributions.
- Provides range of possible outcomes and probabilities + best/worst case scenarios + most likely outcome for event.
- *Advantages:* relatively straightforward method for arriving at likely outcome for uncertain event + confidence limit for outcome; useful for analysing likelihood of meeting project milestones.

11

Risk registers and risk accountability

Risk register: lists all identified risks + result of their analysis and evaluation + information on ownership and status of each risk. Used to track and monitor project risk profile and provide information for further analysis and treatment.

For each identified risk:

- Risk identification number
- Risk type or category
- Date identified
- Risk owner (person responsible for monitoring, overseeing management of risk)
- Description of risk
- Source or cause of risk
- Evaluated probability and cost or impact of risk
- Proposed or selected response actions (if any)
- Current risk status (summary of current position: counter-measures are in place etc)
- Monitoring method and review date and frequency

Register should be **reviewed and amended**:

- As risk mitigation strategies are applied (changing status of risks)
- As new risks are identified
- As required by review and monitoring plans defined for each registered risk

Benefits of risk register:

- Captures all analysis and decisions re identified risks, leading to awareness and accountability
- Provides project sponsor and board with framework for risk status reporting
- Tool for tracking identified risks
- Tool for communication on risk issues with stakeholders
- Can be computerised, aiding analysis, triggering alerts, mitigating action etc.

Managing risk in supply chains

Supply risk: risk associated with an organisation's suppliers (or supply chain) being unable to supply goods of adequate quantity or quality. Eg shortages, quality or labour problems, supplier failure or financial instability, poor supply chain management (eg overly lean supply chains).

Demand risk: risk of unanticipated levels of demand, or demand fluctuations. Eg: price increases, supply shortages, stock-outs. Often caused by poor demand forecasting: need for 'demand management'.

Environmental risks: risks arising in external environment, including eg: terrorism, political unrest, weather, natural disaster. Require environmental scanning and monitoring.

Process and operational risks: risks arising from internal processes (management, operations, back office etc), and decisions about 'core competence': make/do internally, or outsource or subcontract? Process risks include: variation in manufacturing output; poor equipment utilisation; quality failure; warehouse, supply chain or logistics issues; technology failure; loss of customers etc.

Control risks: risks arising from application or misapplication of mechanisms for control.

Creating a supply chain risk management culture

Top management commitment to champion and support risk management throughout the supply chain.

Appreciate importance of proactive risk identification and management in project success and business continuity.

Establish cross-functional project risk team: develop and use risk register; provide regular updates to Board.

OWN NOTES

CHAPTER 12

Methodologies for Planning

Sequencing activities and critical path analysis

Network analysis: analysing relationships between activities and illustrating them as a network to show:

- Precedences and intedependencies (to support sequencing and scheduling)
- Critical activities (where delays will hold up project completion)
- Areas of float or slack time (allowing for slippage, and/or diversion of resources to critical activities to meet deadlines).

Critical path analysis (CPA): shows the network of project activities, identifying the 'critical path': the chain of events with the *longest* duration (ie delay will delay project completion).

Programme analysis and review technique (PERT): uses probability theory to allow for uncertainties in estimated activity durations (best, most likely, worst case) and to calculate the likelihood that activities and/or the whole project will overrun.

Graphical evaluation and review technique (GERT): uses probability theory to allow for uncertainties in outputs and activities (eg failure rates).

Benefits of network analysis

- Enforced need to think clearly about activities, interdependencies and durations
- Focuses attention on 'critical activities', where no slack is available (delay = impact on delivery)
- Identifies potential to shorten total timetable by directing extra resources to critical activities ('crashing' activities)
- Simple tool for monitoring and communicating project progress against schedule
- Potential (eg using PERT) to cope with uncertainties in estimated activity durations.

Preparing a network diagram

- Analyse project activities to derive sequence, relationships
- Draw the network
- Add times for each activity: activity duration (under arrow); Earliest Start Time (EST: upper quadrant of node); and Latest Finish Time (LFT: lower quadrant of node)

12

- Identify the critical path (Longest path: defines project duration. Nodes for which no difference [float] between EST and LFT)
- Schedule activities

Activity	Preceding activities	Duration (days)
A	–	3
B	–	3
C	–	7
D	A	1
E	D, J	2
F	B	2
G	C	1
H	E, F, G	1
J	B	1

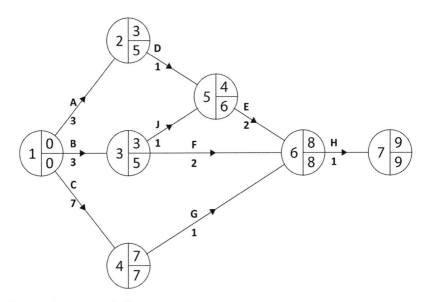

Analysing the network diagram

Total completion time: 9 days

Float for each activity: difference between EST and LFT at each node.

Critical path: activities with no float; longest path to completion (CGH)

'Crashing' activities

If network diagram reveals project is likely to overrun, activities may be **crashed**: duration shortened by applying additional resources.

Identify activities that can be 'crashed'

For each activity, establish cost to crash

Estimate activity duration with resources added

Determine revised completion date and cost

Recalculate critical path and costs

Compare various options for most effective solution

Adding buffers (CCPM)

Buffers: defined quantities of time applied to schedule to protect due date from variation.

- **Feeding buffer**: protects non-critical tasks where they feed into critical tasks.
- **Capacity buffer**: used in programmes, to protect each project from variation in resource use on other projects.
- **Resource buffer**: protects against shortage of key resource when needed.

Gantt charts

Visual timeline for tracking work packages and activities: start and end times, milestones and key dates etc.

Shows planned duration of each task (or product phase) as a line or bar, measured against a scale of hours, days or weeks. Easy-to-view start and end times, overlaps etc.

Personnel and resources required can be plotted for resource planning (where resources need to be allocated, transferred, shared to maximise use)

Actual progress can also be shown against scheduled progress or output, for monitoring and control

Advantages: simple visual tracking of progress and resource requirements; standard information for stakeholder communication.

12

OWN NOTES

CHAPTER 13

Strategic Cost Management

Fixed and variable pricing methods

Contract price adjustment (CPA) clause: provision for upward or downward revision of fixed project price, on occurrence (or non-occurrence) of specified contingencies.

Used to recognise volatile labour or supply market conditions, making firm fixed pricing difficult (and necessitating 'contingency allowances' in contract price)

Price adjustment based on:

- **Actual increases or decreases** in material, labour, commodity or energy costs within life of contract (outside a specified range of variation). Eligible costs and contingency events identified, or subject to negotiation.
- **Links to specified indices:** eg commodities price indices, Labour Market Index (LMI). Index calculations (average changes in cost of items over time) can also be used to estimate average costs; discount inflation; allow for currency fluctuations; compare cost performance of different suppliers over time.
- **CPA formulae** eg BEAMA formula. Total contract price divided into fixed costs, labour, materials. Average materials and labour cost variations calculated using indices, and applied to give total percentage price adjustment.

Budgetary control and variance analysis

Budget: a plan quantified in monetary terms, prepared and approved prior to a defined period of time, usually showing planned or estimated income to be generated and/or expenditure to be incurred during that period, and the capital to be employed to attain a given objective.

13

Budgetary control:

- Establishment of budgets for project or activity, allocated as responsibility of manager or team
- Continuous comparison of actual results (income or costs) with budgeted results
- Identification of variances or deviations; reporting of significant divergences for action.

Supports project management in: planning, co-ordination, communication, motivation, control and performance evaluation.

Approaches to budgeting

Top down: managers use judgement and experience to estimate overall project and work package costs. Project teams are expected to achieve estimated costs in practice.

Bottom up: project teams estimate costs of activities, from which total project cost compiled. (More time-consuming, but more accurate.)

Work element costing: project broken down into work elements; quantities and costs of resources estimated for each work element. Accuracy of estimate depends on validity of assumptions (eg labour hours).

Activity budgeting: project broken down into separate activities; costs for each are estimated (or priced by suppliers) and allocated to relevant week or month of project time-line.

Costing information

Material costs: based on specifications, bill of materials or bill of quantities.

Labour costs: allowed times for each operation, estimated labour hours x rates chargeable for relevant grade of labour (+ travel, subsistence costs, where included).

Overhead rates: separate variable and fixed overhead rates apportioned to cost of activity.

Variances

Variances: differences between budget and actual values. If actual cost less than budget: 'favourable'. If actual cost greater: 'adverse'.

Variance analysis: establish reasons for differences between budgeted and actual costs.
- **Material variances:** price paid (material price variance) and quantity of materials used (material usage variance).
- **Labour variances:** rates of pay (labour price variance) and quantity of labour used (labour usage variance).
- **Overhead variances:** variable overheads and fixed overheads.

Value engineering

Lifecycle costing

More accurate view of total cost of capital assets:
- *Buying costs:* purchase price + other products and services needed + process costs
- *Owning costs:* financing costs + opportunity cost
- *Operating costs:* direct labour + materials and consumables + maintenance
- *Disposal costs:* disposal + environmental compliance

Value engineering

A systematic approach to enhancing the value of a project by seeking **optimal design solutions**, thereby **reducing unnecessary cost,** while maintaining and enhancing all aspects of quality and function.

'Unnecessary cost' of design; components; materials; poor buildability; lifecycle cost. Greatest benefits if applied early in design and specification process.

VE team: appointed by project management; multi-disciplinary (including relevant consultants, contractors)

Methodology:

- *Information phase* (workshops): identify priorities; analyse design features to identify value objectives, cost drivers
- *Speculation phase (*brainstorming): alternative design solutions which fulfil value objectives
- *Evaluation phase:* evaluate proposals for conformance to value objectives; shortlist and rank possible alternative solutions.
- *Development phase:* develop favoured solutions to enable cost studies.
- *Presentation phase:* recommendations to design team and project manager.
- *Implementation of VE proposals:* if accepted, project manager indicates where recommendations incorporated into design, with cost/time implications; consults project sponsor on changes to project brief.

Consortium-based procurement

Buying alliance: 'Two or more organisations, or groups within organisations, collaborating on certain aspects of spend to generate leverage and better VFM for all.' (CIPS)

Consolidated buying: organisations purchasing together *or* joint ventures. Alliances may be:

- 'Vertical': organisations in same industry sector buying things specific to sector
- 'Horizontal': organisations in different sectors buying things common to all sectors
- 'Intra-organisational': groupings within same organisation or group, buying together
- 'Inter-organisational': different or competing companies, industries or organisations.

Strategic framework contracts ('collaborative contracts') for PPM: term contracts let for grouped requirements across a range of organisations. Fewer contracts and more controlled, rationalised supply chains.

Benefits of consortium purchasing: leverage; volume discounts; reduced acquisition costs; shared market intelligence; shared resources; investment in market development; increased supplier interest; coherent communication; procurement focus on more strategic procurement; inter-member trading to cover shortages.

Disadvantages of consortium purchasing: central purchasing organisation needs to recover

13

process costs (mark-up charged to tendered prices contracted with suppliers); non-mandatory (lack of buy-in); lack of co-ordination or trust between members. Can erode potential savings.

Open book costing and cost transparency

Open-book costing: purchasers have access to supplier costing information: mechanisms for checking contractor's costs and margins.

- Increasingly adopted in construction industry. Linked to use of cost-reimburseable and target cost pricing mechanisms. NEC: project manager entitled to inspect contractor's records re payments of defined costs, proof of payments, subcontractor variations etc.
- *Advantages:* reassures re VFM (not exploitative profit margins); facilitates cost-based pricing; enables buyer to get to know supplier operations and processes; enables identification of areas for cost reduction, value addition
- *Disadvantages:* flow of costing information is one-way (reflecting buyer dominance); risk to commercially sensitive information; suppliers may protect interests by providing inaccurate data; parties may not share value added (in adversarial relationship).

Cost transparency: purchaser and supplier share two-way process and cost information, for activities in which they have a common interest.

- *Objective:* reduce costs through joint development of good ideas, improving mutual competitive position of both firms (Lamming)
- *Advantages:* enables identification of areas for cost reduction; enables mutual understanding of objectives, constraints; encourages collaboration for mutual benefit; suits strategic or partnership relationships (with confidentiality protection).

OWN NOTES

OWN NOTES

CHAPTER 14

Financial and Management Information

Estimating budgets

Bases for cost estimation:

- Availability of funds (eg budget allocations)
- Estimated costs associated with defined project activities (labour + cost of materials + overheads)
- Estimated prices from suppliers and contractors (including contract management, financing etc): importance of 'market dialogue'.
- Historical data (costs of past similar activities) + market intelligence (eg trends and influences on prices) + statistical techniques (eg weighted average, trend analysis, regression analysis)

Measurement, monitoring, control and improvement

Progress monitoring: reviewing monthly progress reports produced by project team.

- May focus on critical activities and variance reporting (reporting by exception)
- Progress reports to sponsor: overall status and rate of progress (realism of forecast completion date and costs); problems (and options for resolution).
- Information for decision-making; assurance that management systems and controls are operating effectively; discipline for project team.

Measures of progress: percentage completion (cost or time); planned v actual; work in progress; impact on critical path; payment progress; overall work content; outstanding requirements.

Time control:

- Time budget (project duration as fixed by constraints)
- Time plan (allowances for activities, ie schedule)
- Time checking (actual time spent v time plan; variance reporting)
- Remedial action for critical activity overrun: re-sequence later activities; 'crash' future activities.

14

Cost control:

- Costs estimated and captured in project budget
- As expenditure incurred, allocated to account codes set up in budget
- Comparison of actual v budgeted expenditure, investigation of variances

Change control:

- Changes to design or specification are key cause of budget and schedule variances
- Changes arise from: unclear project definition, poor communication, lack of planning and risk management – *or* changing circumstances or contingencies.
- Identified potential changes should be treated as project risk.
- Need for robust change control procedures, incorporating VFM criteria.

Project tracking and control mechanisms

Reporting and control

Project reporting system should be:

- Designed to meet needs of all stakeholders
- Tied in with WBS, so relevant to control of specific tasks or schedule
- Timed to correspond to project milestones.

Benefits of timely and targeted reports: mutual understanding of goals; awareness of progress; realistic planning; understanding independencies; early warning of problems and faster response; higher visibility to top management; keeping client and stakeholders up to date.

Problems in preparation of reports: too much detail; poor interface between client and project IT systems; poor correspondence between planning and reporting systems.

Objectives of control systems:

- Regulation of results (through alteration of activities)
- Stewardship of organisational assets

Earned value analysis (EVA)

Apparent on-target costs may disguise fact that activities *have not been completed*: need to integrate time and cost measures for EVA.

Control system assessing *actual work* and *completed value of work* against plan, to see if project is on track:

- Integrates cost, schedule and scope measures
- Can be used to forecast future performance
- Provides early warning of cost and schedule problems.

Earned value: how much budget or time *should have been spent* (according to plan) for *amount of work done*.

- Budgeted cost of work scheduled (BCWS) or planned value (PV): amount *budgeted* to be spent *at this point in the schedule*.
- Budgeted cost of work performed (BCWP) or earned value (EV): amount *budgeted* for *work actually completed* to date.
- Actual cost of work performed (ACWP) or actual cost (AC): *actual cost* incurred in work actually performed to date.
- BCWP *minus* ACWP = **cost variance** (CV): +ve = within budget; −ve = overrun. May also be calculated as ratio: Cost Performance Index (CPI) – less than 1.0 = overrun.
- BCWP *minus* BCWS = **schedule variance** (SV): +ve = ahead; −ve = behind. May also be calculated as ratio: Schedule Performance Index (SPI) to show rate of progress.
- Use S curve to plot values

Controlling variations

Causes of variations:

- Change of specification or scope
- Change of schedule
- Financial problems
- Inadequate project objectives (leading to scope creep)
- Lowest price procurement processes (leading to variations used to claw back costs)

NEC3 contracts:

- Pre-defined 'compensation events' (for which variations allowable)
- Early Warning Notices re matters which could increase contract price or cause delays
- Risk Register and Reduction Meetings to mitigate effects of emerging circumstances which might necessitate variations

Implementing remedial actions

Powers of project manager (NEC3 terms):

- Early warning of events that could cause variation
- Instruct contractor to attend risk reduction meeting
- Stop or not start any work
- Submit quotations for acceleration of work
- Order contractor to correct defects
- Re-contract defect rectification to third party, if not carried out by contractor
- Approve quotations for compensation events
- Decide to terminate contract

Alternative dispute resolution (ADR) – as an alternative to litigation (court-based resolution of contractual disputes): negotiation, mediation, conciliation, neutral evaluation, expert determination, adjudication, arbitration.

14

OWN NOTES

CHAPTER 15

Implications of Performance Issues

Consequential losses and damages

Breach of contract: a party to a contract fails or refuses to do what they are obligated to do under the contract. Injured party can claim **damages.**

Purpose of damages: financial compensation for loss suffered as a result of breach – aiming to put injured party in same position as if breach had not occurred.

Unliquidated damages: contract makes no provision for fixed amount of damages; court determines damages. Claimant must show that they have suffered a loss *and:*

- The loss was **consequential** and not too **remote** from the breach *[Hadley v Baxendale]*:
  - Caused 'naturally' in the course of business by the breach – *or*
  - A 'reasonably foreseeable' result of the breach – depending on any special knowledge possessed by parties, but regardless of whether the extent of the damage was foreseen.
  - Not necessarily including lost profits *[Victoria Laundry v Newman Industries]*
- The **measure** or amount of damages is reasonable: an amount which will, so far as money can, put the claimant in the same position as if contract had been performed.
  - If no actual loss suffered, nominal *[Surrey CC v Bredero Homes]*
  - Claimant must take reasonable steps to avoid or minimise ('mitigate') loss *[Payzu v Saunders]*

Liquidated damages and penalties

Liquidated damages: contract expressly provides for fixed sum on breach.

- Must be genuine attempt to estimate loss *[Dunlop Pneumatic Tyre Co v New Garage]* – *not* a 'penalty clause' (sum does not distinguish between small and large breaches; clause imposed post-contract; sum extravagant: *Aflred McALpine Capital Projects v Tilebox]*
- Injured party can *only* claim liquidated amount *[Cellulose Acetate Slik Co v Widnes Foundry]*.

15

Common liquidated damages clauses for:

- Delay (eg NEC3 'delay damages)
- Inefficiency of completed works or poor service levels (eg 'service credits'): common eg in IT service provision contracts

Service credits: pre-specified financial amounts, to which client becomes entitled if agreed service levels are not achieved (as defined in contract or SLA: eg response times).

- Mechanism eg: % rebates (per % service shortfall) *or* points accumulation.
- Contract may stipulate *not* a form of liquidated damages, but a mechanism for varying service charges according to different levels of performance. (Remedies not constrained by need to estimate losses.)
- Parties may agree a 'termination threshold', based on the level of service credits accrued over a specified period, giving a right of termination in the face of persistent defaults.

Contractual warranties and conditions

Conditions are vital terms of a contract: breach entitles wronged party to 'repudiate' (cancel) the contract + damages for losses suffered *[Poussard v Spiers, 1876]*

Warranties are non-vital terms of contract: breach only entitles wronged party to damages: mutual obligations remain in place *[Bettini v Gye, 1876]*

Innominate (intermediate) terms: may be treated as a condition or warranty *depending* on the effect of breach *[Hong Kong Fir Shipping Co v Kawasaki, 1962]*

Specific performance

Equitable remedy whereby court orders defendant to carry out obligations under contract, as alternative to damages.

Will NOT be ordered:

- Where plaintiff is seeking to exploit harsh contract terms (not 'in good faith')
- Where damages are an adequate remedy (eg to cover non-rectification of defects)
- Where the court could not adequately supervise performance of the contract.

Termination clauses

Contractual provisions for termination

Contract **discharged** by performance of works stipulated. Projects: completion through 'substantial performance' (only sight variances, omissions, defects: *Hoenig v Isaacs).*

Duration clause: specifying contract period, with commencement and expiry dates.

Termination for default clause: allowing termination in case of material default or breach (eg substantial failure to comply with obligations; not provided required bond or guarantee; appointed subcontractor without approval: NEC3)

Determination clause (or 'forfeiture clause'): either or both parties entitled to terminate contract in specified circumstances (eg delay, lack of due diligence, insolvency).

Termination for convenience (or 'break provision'): allowing termination 'at will' or 'for convenience'. May need to justify reasons as 'rational, honest and proper' and provide for contractor compensation on *quantum meruit* basis. May not be used to obtain better price from another contractor *[Abbey Development v PP Brickwork, 2003]*

Quantum meruit

Equitable remedy where a contract has been part-performed: reasonable sum to be paid for services rendered or work done, if amount due not expressly stated in contract *[ERDC Group v Brunel University]*: '*quantum meruit*' = 'what it is worth'.

Performance bonds and guarantees

Performance bond: sum of money set aside as a guarantee of satisfactory completion of a project by a contractor eg surety bond or bank guarantee. Client is guaranteed payment up to stated amount (eg 10% of contract sum) if he suffers loss as result of contractor default or breach.

Parent company guarantee: contractor's immediate parent or other holding company agrees to guarantee (stand surety for) liability of contractor for debt or default. If contractor is no longer able or willing to continue works, parent must complete works to standard specified in original contract.

Frustration

Frustration: contract terminated where intervening circumstances prevent performance as intended (further performance impossible, illegal or radically different from what was contemplated), without default of either party.

- Eg: destruction of subject matter; incapacity; change in law; extensive interruption – but NOT contract simply becoming more difficult or expensive to perform than anticipated *[Davis Contractors v Fareham Urban District Council]*
- Contract automatically ends and parties excused from *future* obligations (but accrued liabilities remain).

Force majeure: 'any circumstances beyond reasonable control of a party which prevent or impede the due performance of a contract including war or hostilities; riot or civil commotion; epidemic; earthquake flood or other natural disaster' (IChemE)

Force majeure clause in contract expressly releases parties from liability where default results from *force majeure* events.

15

OWN NOTES

CHAPTER 16

The Closure of Major Programmes and Projects

Obtaining client acceptance and installing deliverables

'Deliverable': quantifiable (tangible or intangible) goods or services to be provided on completion.

- Each deliverable should be assigned to a separate phase of the project.
- Similar deliverables, involving same team and stakeholders: group together in phase
- Deliverables worked on during same time period: group into phases.

'Quality' in projects: 'issue that affects the project so that work needs to be redone, modified or compromised to a lesser standard than was originally agreed'.

- *Rejection:* work deemed unreasonable, work has to be completely restarted
- *Rework:* work requries modification to return to agreed standard
- *Compromise:* project team accepts work below agreed standard.

Key performance indicators

KPIs: used to measure deliverables + enable stakeholders to understand performance levels.

Key stages of project (for KPI definition): Commit to invest; Commit to construct; Available for use; End of defect liability period; End of lifetime.

Sample KPIs:

- *Time*: time for completion; time predictability (design, construction, design + contruction); time to rectify defects
- *Cost:* cost for completion; cost predictability (design, construction, design + construction); cost to rectify defects
- *Quality:* defects; quality defects at 'available for use'; quality defects at 'end of defect liability period'
- *Client satisfaction:* client satisfaction with delivered product; client satisfaction with service
- *Health and safety:* reported accidents; lost time due to accidents.

16

Conducting project audits

Three dimensions to audit:
- *Efficiency* (conformance to budget and schedule)
- *Customer impact* (conformance to specifications; customer satisfaction)
- *Business/direct success* (contribution to objectives eg market share)

Benefits of recommendations from project audit: early problem identification; clarify performance, cost and time relationships; identification of potential for innovation; evaluation of project management; cost reduction; improved risk management; identification of mistakes for remedying and future avoidance.

Template for project audit:
- **Introduction**: (project, objectives, key stakeholders)
- **Current status**: cost (v budget); schedule (v milestones); quality (v specification)
- **Future project status** (recommendations for future projects)
- **Management issues** (relationships in project team and supply chain)
- **Risk management** (major risks; impact on time, performance and cost; risk management)

Steps for effective auditing (Walker & Bracey):
- Small team of experienced experts.
- Familiarise team with project requirements.
- Audit project on site.
- Debrief project management.
- Written report; pre-specified format.
- Distribute report to project manager and team for response.
- Follow up to ensure recommendations implemented.

Knowledge management

Knowledge management: organisation, creation, sharing and flow of knowledge within organisations.

Objective: optimise knowledge available to organisation; create new knowledge; increase awareness and understanding. Identification, capture and transfer of learning (a) from one project to another and (b) from sharing of project management best practice.

David Kolb: importance of learning by doing + reflection (experiential learning cycle)

Nonaka &Takeuchi: organisational learning results from 'knowledge conversion':
- **Individual knowledge** being captured, transferred, enlarged and shared upwards to the organisational level
- Exploiting of both **tacit** knowledge (unarticulated insight, intuition, 'know-how') + **explicit** knowledge (objective, factual)

	Tacit	Tacit	
Tacit	**SOCIALISATION** **From tacit to tacit** Sharing experiences, mental models and skills	**EXTERNALISATION** **From tacit to explicit** Articulating tacit knowledge into concepts	**Explicit**
Tacit	**INTERNALISATION** **From explicit to tacit** Embodying explicit knowledge into tacit knowledge	**COMBINATION** **From explicit to explicit** Systemising concepts into known systems	**Explicit**
	Explicit	Explicit	

Communicating the review, evaluation and learning

Improving knowledge management:

- Encourage knowledge sharing between client, project team and supply chain
- Communication of post-completion audit and debrief by project manager.
- Capture (eg database) of learning from past projects
- Development and use of shared IT systems; disseminate learning and best practice (eg intranet, extranet)
- Interest groups and knowledge communities (sharing feedback and learning)
- Bodies of knowledge eg: Project Management Body of Knowledge (PMBOK), PRINCE2 guidelines for good practice
- Benchmarking of project performance against eg excellence standards.

Managing negative feedback:

- Encourage openness and expression of conflicts
- Role model resolution processes
- Demonstrate harnessing of conflict to achieve positive outcomes: learning from mistakes

OWN NOTES